The Little Book of Sequencing Skills

by Keri Finlayson
Illustrations by Mike Phillips

LITTLE IDEAS

Published 2013, by Featherstone Education.
an imprint of Bloomsbury Publishing Plc
50 Bedford Square, London, WC1B 3DP
www.bloomsbury.com

ISBN 978-1-4081-8029-7

Text © Keri Finlayson
Illustrations ©Mike Phillips/Beehive Illustration
Cover photographs © Shutterstock

Printed in Great Britain by Latimer Trend & Company Limited

10 9 8 7 6 5 4 3 2 1

This book is produced using paper that is made from wood grown in
managed, sustainable forests. It is natural, renewable and recyclable.
The logging and manufacturing processes conform to the environmental
regulations of the country of origin.

**To see our full range of titles
visit www.bloomsbury.com**

Contents

Introduction

The ability to sequence events and objects and put thoughts and actions into sequence are essential for children's early development. Sequencing skills are often associated with Communication and Language and Literacy but the ability to predict what will come next – whether it be in a mathematical pattern, following instructions, understanding patterns of letters and sounds, or understanding the consequences of actions – is fundamental to all areas of early learning.

The Little Book of Sequencing Skills provides early years practitioners with a variety of practical and creative ways to teach the children in their care to recognise and create sequences and to do so within the context of a variety of areas of learning.

Sequencing skills and the EYFS

PRIME AREAS

Communication and Language

In order to be able to communicate our thoughts clearly we need to be able to express them in a logical order. The ability to place events in sequence helps children to think clearly and enables them to express their thoughts and wishes logically in a way which is understandable to others. This is a skill that can be built on, and once mastered can have a profound effect on later communication skills. The child who can present their thoughts and views clearly, calmly, and in order is a more confident child and a more successful communicator.

Sequencing encourages comprehension and critical thinking skills. If we are familiar with the idea of cause and effect, that one event necessarily follows another, then the motivations of characters in a story become more understandable.

Sequencing identifies the components of a story – the beginning, middle and the end – and enables children to retell the events in the order in which they occurred. This encourages both story comprehension and story creation.

Physical development

Gross and fine motor skills are practised through sequencing skills, whether used during construction activities, travelling games or fine motor activities such as cutting or threading. From following simple sewing patterns to travelling across a space using a sequence of movements, young children's physical development is enhanced by putting movements in order.

Personal and Social Development

Sequencing activities enable a child to comprehend and then to predict consequences of actions – their own and those of others. This is an important social skill. If I take a toy away from someone then they will feel sad; if I share, the consequence is that we are both happy. For the very young, this understanding of the consequences of social behaviour takes explicit instruction and, for many, lots of practice.

Sequencing skills are essential for learning tasks such as preparing food, dressing and self care. A recipe must be followed step by step, we have to put our socks on before our shoes and it is helpful to brush our teeth in a sequence to ensure effective cleaning. All these sequencing skills may seem obvious to an adult but are absolutely essential to a young child's development.

The ability to understand and predict sequences is essential in developing problem solving skills in a multitude of real life situations that involve instructions and directions. In order to follow directions we have to follow and remember step by step instructions and to understand the importance and relevance of that order.

SPECIFIC AREAS

Literacy

A child's 'reading and writing readiness' – the acquisition of a range of skills necessary to begin reading and writing – is grounded in sequencing skills. Children need to understand that patterns of sounds exist and that sounds follow patterns of letters.

Mathematics

Sequencing is fundamental to mathematics. Sequencing skills are necessary in order to place objects in order of size and to spot numerical patters. They are fundamental to understanding notions of size, progression, comparison and quantity.

Understanding the world

Sequencing skills are necessary for understanding the world around us. The life cycle of plants and the growth and development of animals and humans all take place in sequence. Time is a progression; a sequence of events. From parts of the day and days of the week to months of the year and the seasons, sequences are the way in which we mark time. In order to do this, children learn the names we give these events and the order in which they come.

Expressive arts and design

Sequencing skills are necessary for creative appreciation, expression and performance in a range of expressive arts.

Appreciating and creating music requires the prediction and reproduction of melodic and rhythmic patterns. By learning to follow musical patterns children can become music makers themselves. With this understanding of the patterns and sequences that make music, children can go on to reproduce music created by others.

Dance is the production of sequences of movement both stationary and travelling. Learning to dance is a wonderful skill; one that children love to learn. Good for physical development as well as cognitive development, learning the steps of a dance is one of the best ways for young children to develop sequencing skills.

Craft and design involves the planning and constructing of visual art. All artistic practice involves planning, whether it be thinking of an idea, or organising materials and equipment. Craft and design in the early years involves facilitating children's exposure to a wide range of craft materials and then showing the sequence of actions necessary to create artefacts and images.

Using this book

The activities and suggestions in this book will help you and the children in your care to explore a range of creative ideas to develop sequencing skills. Designed for children in the Foundation Stage, all the activities can be carried out as they are laid out or can be adapted according to your children's aptitudes and needs. Children have varying attention spans; you can shorten, lengthen or adapt the activities according to your professional judgement.

The book is organized into six topic sections: Fairytales and Nursery rhymes; Life skills; Growth, development and time; Physical development and movement; Art and design; and Music and dance. Each of the topics contains a range of activities whose outcomes are drawn from across the EYFS seven areas of learning. The activities are designed to be cross-curricular – referencing themes from mathematics to expressive arts, literacy to physical development.

The materials needed are listed at the beginning of each activity, most items are to be found in any early years setting.

Talking is an important part of early learning and for this reason many of the activities are accompanied by a 'Tips for talk' section. These sections offer the practitioner suggestions for exploratory talk; conversations that lead to a deeper understanding of the purpose of the sequencing topic. Exploratory, open ended talk is a great way for a child to place the topic in the context of their everyday life and to understand how the sequencing skills being developed are relevant to their experience. Talking about a topic also affords the practitioner the opportunity for informal assessment; to gauge a child's comprehension of the topic being explored.

Many of the activities include additional ideas (And another idea) to extend the learning.

Fairytales

Understanding that a story is made up from a sequence of events both develops comprehension skills and encourages children to make their own stories. Story sequencing also teaches children about the jobs that words do and how those words move a narrative forward. Fairytales are ideal for creating sequencing activities. These types of tales often have repeated themes and motifs that move the action from initial premise to conclusion.

The activities in this section are centered on four popular fairytales. The tales have been abridged with the sequence of events emphasised.

▶ Goldilocks and the Three Bears
▶ The Three Little Pigs
▶ Red Riding Hood
▶ Jack and the Beanstalk

Nursery rhymes

Children love nursery rhymes. Their simple structure and repetitive pattern makes them ideal for helping very young children to recognise and learn sequences in sounds and letters and also predict what comes next.

Have fun reciting the following nursery rhymes together and then support the children in the related activities which enhance other areas of learning as well as developing sequencing skills.

▶ Hickory Dickory Dock

▶ Hey Diddle Diddle

▶ Little Miss Muffet

▶ Humpty Dumpty

Goldilocks and the Three Bears

Goldilocks went into the cottage and saw three bowls of porridge.
She tried the biggest bowl. It was too hot!
She tried the middle sized bowl. It was too cold!
She tried the little bowl and it was just right so she ate it all up!

Goldilocks looked for somewhere to sit.
The first chair was too big.
The second chair was also too big.
Goldilocks sat down in the third chair. It broke!

Goldilocks saw three beds.
She lay on the first. It was too hard.
She lay on the second. It was too soft.
She lay on the third and fell asleep.

The three bears returned.
Daddy Bear said. 'Who's been eating my porridge?'
Mummy Bear said, 'Who's been eating my porridge?'
Baby Bear said, 'Someone's been eating my porridge and it's all gone!'

Daddy bear said, 'Someone's been sitting in my chair.'
Mummy Bear said, 'Someone's been sitting in my chair.'
Baby Bear said, 'Someone's been sitting in my chair and it's broken.'

They went upstairs.
Daddy Bear said, 'Someone's been sleeping in my bed.'
Mummy Bear said, 'Someone's been sleeping in my bed.'
Baby Bear said, 'Someone's been sleeping in my bed and they're still there!'
Goldilocks leapt up, ran downstairs and never came back to the cottage again!

Goldilocks' lucky dip

Sequence the story of Goldilocks by picking items from a fairytale lucky dip and placing them in order.

What you need:

▶ three small plastic bowls and spoons
▶ three small world chairs (dolls' house or similar)
▶ three small world blankets and pillows (or scraps of fabric)
▶ a pile of old newspapers
▶ sellotape and scissors
▶ a large box or plastic tub
▶ three teddy bears
▶ a doll (Goldilocks)

What you do:

1. Wrap the bowls and spoons, the small world chairs, tables and beds/blankets and pillows in newspaper and place in the box or plastic tub.
2. Fill the tub with shredded or crumpled newspaper and place the bears and Goldilocks doll in front of the box.
3. Gather the children round and read the story of Goldilocks on the previous page.
4. Revisit and recall the events of the story with the children. Talk about the objects in the story.
5. Ask each child to pick out an object from the 'lucky dip' and unwrap it.
6. Place each object in front of 'Goldilocks and the three bears'. Once all the objects have been unwrapped, help the children to arrange them in the correct order of events from left to right.

And another idea:

▶ Ask two or three children to re-enact the story using the props.
▶ Use the props and toys for observational drawing, sequencing the completed pictures.

Tips for talk:

▶ Have you ever eaten porridge? Do you like it?
▶ Why were the bears cross with Goldilocks?
▶ Was Goldilocks wrong to eat their food?
▶ Where is your favourite place to sit?

The Three Little Pigs

Once upon a time there were three little pigs who decided to build their own houses.

The first little pig built a house of straw.
The second little pig built a house of sticks.
The third little pig built a house of bricks.

One night a wolf came to the straw house.
He said, 'Little pig, Little pig let me come in'.
The pig said, 'Not by the hair of my chinny chin chin'.
The wolf said, 'Then I'll huff and I'll puff and I'll blow your house down'.
And he ate the pig up.

The wolf came to the stick house.
He said, 'Little pig, little pig let me come in'.
The pig said, 'Not by the hair of my chinny chin chin.'
The wolf said, 'Then I'll huff and I'll puff and I'll blow your house down'.
And he ate the pig up.

The wolf came to the brick house.
He said, 'Little pig, little pig let me come in'.
The pig said, 'Not by the hair of my chinny chin chin.'
The wolf said, 'Then I'll huff and I'll puff and I'll blow your house down.'
But he couldn't because the house was so strong. So he went away hungry.

Pasta house triptych

Make a triptych (picture in 3 sections) showing the three different types of houses in the story of The Three Little Pigs.

What you need:

- angel hair pasta broken into 3cm pieces (straw house)
- spaghetti broken into 5cm pieces (stick house)
- macaroni or other small pasta shapes (brick house)
- PVA glue and A5 card
- glue spreaders or brushes

What you do:

1. Read the story of The Three Little Pigs.
2. Discuss the three types of building material (see 'Tips for talk').
3. Divide the A5 paper into three equal vertical sections and draw a simple outline of a house in each section.
4. Ask the children to make a picture of the straw house in the first section by gluing the angel hair pasta onto the outline of the house. In the second section ask them to use the pieces of spaghetti to make the stick house, in the third section use macaroni to represent the brick house.

And another idea:

- Make houses out of other materials such as wooden or plastic blocks, boxes or paper/card.
- Find pictures of houses from around the world. What are they made from?

Tips for talk:

- The wolf found the house of straw easiest to blow down. Why do you think that was?
- What is your house made from? Who built it?

Little Red Riding Hood

Once upon a time a little girl called Little Red Riding Hood took some cakes to her poorly grandmother.

On the way through the forest she met a wolf. The wolf asked her where she was going. She said, 'I'm going to Granny's house'.

The wolf rushed ahead to Granny's house and ate Granny up! He put on Granny's clothes and got into her bed.

Little Red Riding Hood came to the cottage and went inside.
She said to the wolf in the bed, 'Oh Granny what big eyes you have!'
'All the better to see you with,' said the wolf.

Then she said, 'Oh Granny what a big nose you have!'
'All the better to smell you with,' said the wolf.

Finally she said, 'Oh Granny what big teeth you have!'
'All the better to eat you with,' said the wolf.
And he jumped at Little Red Riding Hood.

Just then a woodcutter ran through the door.
He chopped the wolf in two and out popped Granny.
The woodcutter, Granny and Little Red Riding Hood had the cakes for tea.

Red Riding Hood's basket

Fill Red Riding Hood's basket with items from the story, then place them in the right order.

What you need:

▶ a picnic basket
▶ a red headscarf
▶ a wolf mask
▶ shawl, blanket or large scarf
▶ flash cards x 3: 1 x picture of eyes, 1 x mouth, 1 x wolf ears

What you do:

1. Read the story with the children and discuss the events.

2. Show the children the props and give them time to explore them independently.

3. After the children have familiarised themselves with the objects put all the props in the basket.

4. Now ask the children to take one item at a time out of the basket. Ask them to place the items in the correct order they appear in the story. Prompt children by asking if the item comes before or after the previous one.

And another idea:

▶ Use the props to act out the story.
▶ Make food items from dough and create a perfect picnic basket full of things that the children like to eat.

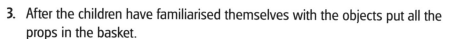

Tips for talk:

▶ Do you have relatives that you visit? Do you ever bring them food/gifts?
▶ What would be in your perfect picnic basket?

Jack and the Beanstalk

Once upon a time there was a poor boy called Jack.
His mother told him to take their cow to market to sell.
On the way there he met a man who bought the cow for some magic beans.
Jack took the beans home but his mother was very cross.
She threw the beans on the ground.
A beanstalk grew up into the clouds.
Jack climbed the beanstalk and found a giant's castle.
He crept into the castle and stole some gold coins.
Next he stole a goose that laid golden eggs.
Then he stole a magic harp that played itself.
The giant tried to come down the beanstalk to catch Jack.
But Jack chopped the beanstalk down with an axe.

The beanstalk frieze

Make a giant beanstalk for your wall. Place the characters from the story as they appear.

What you need:

▶ green frieze paper
▶ scissors
▶ glue
▶ A4 paper
▶ sticky tack
▶ pictures of: a cow, some beans, a bean stalk and clouds, a castle, gold coins, golden egg, harp, axe

What you do:

1. Make a giant beanstalk for your wall by first, cutting eight large leaf shapes (approx 10-15cm in length) from the green frieze paper.

2. Make a stem from the paper approx 5cm x 1m long.

3. Fix the stem to the wall using sticky tack, positioning and sticking the leaves alternately up both sides of the stem.

4. Now make the pictures for the children to choose and stick on the beanstalk. Draw the eight items from the story (listed and shown on the opposite page) or find suitable images from magazines or the internet.

5. Glue the pictures to the backing card and cut out.

6. Read the story of Jack and the Beanstalk with the children.

7. Show them the eight objects that feature in the story and discuss their order of appearance.

8. Using sticky tack, help children to fix the objects onto the giant beanstalk leaves, the first to appear (the cow) on the lowest leaf, the last to appear (the axe) on the highest leaf.

And another idea:

▶ Plant your own beans. If you have outside space plant runner beans in the ground. If space is limited why not plant beans in a deep pot and place near the front door of your setting?

Hickory dickory dock

Hickory dickory dock
The mouse ran up the clock
The clock struck one
The mouse ran down
Hickory dickory dock

Hickory dickory dare
The pig flew up in the air
The man in brown
Soon brought him down
Hickory dickory dare

Up and Down

Hickory Dickory Dock is all about ups and downs. Be lively mice and busy pigs and follow a sequence of up and down movements. This activity is pretty tricky but is lots and lots of fun!

What you need:

▶ a whiteboard or chalk board
▶ pens or chalks
▶ simple cardboard mouse and pig masks (optional)

What you do:

1. First read the rhyme.
2. Divide the children into two groups, pigs and mice. If you have made animal masks, give each group their masks to put on. Ensure the eye holes are large enough for the children to see!
3. Read the first verse again – the mice stand up then sit down.
4. Read the second verse – the pigs stand up then sit down.
5. Now create a sequence of mice and pigs 'ups' and 'downs'.
6. Write a large 'm' on the board and explain to the children that this represents 'mice'.
7. Write a large 'p' on the board and explain to the children that this represents 'pigs'.
8. Draw an arrow pointing up and an arrow pointing down.
9. Now using these symbols, display a short sequence on the board. Point to each symbol in turn and see if the mice and pigs can follow it. For example: m – ↑. m – ↓. m – ↑. p – ↑. p – ↓. p – ↑.

And another idea:

▶ Add other simple movements. Decide on symbols for these movements together and add them to the sequence. e.g. a circle could mean 'turn around', a zig zag could mean 'jump'.

Hey diddle diddle

Hey diddle diddle
The cat and the fiddle
The cow jumped over the moon
The little dog laughed to see such fun
And the dish ran away with the spoon

The diddle muddle

There are four action scenes in the rhyme 'Hey diddle diddle'. Try this sequencing activity (with a twist) that makes simple sequencing cards into something quite different. Children pick cards from one of four bags at different places in the rhyme making a hilariously different version of events.

What you need:

▶ 4 bags labelled A, B , C, D (If you don't have suitable bags, boxes are fine)

▶ 16 blank sequencing cards (approx. 8cm x 6cm)

What you do:

1. Draw or cut and paste the following images onto the 16 cards and then sort the cards into four groups – A, B, C, D.

Group A	Group B	Group C	Group D
fiddle	moon	dog	spoon
trumpet	sun	duck	cup
drum	house	horse	knife
triangle	mountain	lion	fork

2. Place each group of cards into the corresponding bag, i.e. Group A cards go into the bag labelled A, Group B cards go into the bag labelled B, and so on.
3. Recite the rhyme together.
4. Now recite the rhyme again, this time choosing a card from one of the bags at a key place, naming the object as you do so:

Hey diddle diddle the cat and the .... (card from Bag A)

The cow jumped over the ..... (card from Bag B)

The little ..... (card from Bag C) laughed to see such fun

And the dish ran away with the .... (card from Bag D)

And another idea:

▶ Can you think of some even sillier items to place in the rhyme? The cow jumped over the... teapot? The dish ran away with the... yellow digger?

Little Miss Muffet

Little Miss Muffet
Sat on a tuffet,
Eating some curds and whey.
Along came a spider
Who sat down beside her,
And frightened Miss Muffet away.

Little Miss Muffet and the silly spider

This silly spider keeps turning up in the wrong rhyme at the wrong time. Children use their prediction skills to decide when the right time is for him to appear.

What you need:

- ▶ large black woolen pom poms
- ▶ black pipe cleaners
- ▶ elastic
- ▶ googly eyes
- ▶ PVA glue

What you do:

1. Make a spider by attaching eight pipe cleaner legs to the pom pom body. Add googly eyes and thread the elastic through the centre of the pom pom body and affix.

2. Recite the rhyme with the children. When you reach the line 'along came a spider' dangle the spider in front of the children.

3. Explain that this spider sometimes gets things wrong and appears in the wrong rhyme. He should only appear after the words 'curds and whey'. Tell the children to listen very carefully – if he appears after any other foods they should wag their fingers at him and he will go away. If he appears in the correct rhyme they should clap. Here are some suggestions for wrong rhymes:

Little Miss Muffet
Sat on a tuffet
Eating some... toast and jam.

Little Miss Muffet
Sat on a tuffet
Eating some... sausage and mash.

Little Miss Muffet
Sat on a tuffet
Eating some... chicken and rice.

And another idea:

▶ Make spiders with the children. Let the children hold their spiders while reciting the rhyme. Tell them that their spiders must appear on their threads whenever they hear the words 'curds and whey'.

Humpty Dumpty

Humpty Dumpty sat on a wall.
Humpty Dumpty had a great fall.
All the king's horses and all the king's men
couldn't put Humpty together again.

Humpty Dumpty jigsaw

The king's horses and the king's men couldn't put Humpty together again but you can put this puzzle together and put the rhyme in the right order.

What you need:

▶ 4 x pieces of thin card
▶ a laminator
▶ scissors
▶ pens
▶ a box or bag for storage

What you do:

1. The rhyme Humpty Dumpty can be divided into four scenes. Draw simple sketches (or use computer images) of each of the below scenes on the pieces of card. Laminate the cards if possible.

   1. Humpty on a wall.
   2. Humpty broken on the ground.
   3. The king's horses and men.
   4. The king's horses and men and broken Humpty.

2. To make the sequencing puzzle cut interlocking jigsaw shapes on one side of each card so when the cards are placed in the correct sequence they fit together.

3. Recite the rhyme together.

4. Ask the children to complete the sequencing jigsaw.

And another idea:

▶ Act out the rhyme using finger puppets.

▶ Make your own Humptys by decorating hard boiled eggs.

Topic Two

Life skills

Being organised is an important part of life. In order to become organised we need to develop good habits and routines. Many of our daily routines are sequences. This section on life skills provides activities containing simple sequencing steps that will develop children's confidence and skill in achieving simple daily tasks.

▶ A little bit of toast (making breakfast)

▶ Starting the day in a positive way!

▶ Following a simple recipe

▶ The toothbrush boogie (brushing teeth)

▶ The great sock race (taking shoes and socks on and off)

A little bit of toast

Which goes on first, butter or jam? Even the simplest of recipes must happen in sequence.

What you need:

- slices of bread (real or pretend)
- knives (plastic)
- pot of real jam or pot of pretend jam
- tub of margarine or butter (empty if role playing)
- plates
- real or toy toaster (if using real toaster follow safety guidelines)

What you do:

1. Discuss what the children have for breakfast.
2. Talk about the steps you take to make toast, stressing toaster safety issues!
3. Place the real or pretend food and cutlery in a line in order of use.
4. Which goes on first butter or jam?
5. Have fun making and eating the yummy toast and jam!

Starting the day in a positive way!

Our morning routines may vary slightly but we all need to get ready. Put your tasks in order and get organised for the day!

What you need:

- a toothbrush
- a hairbrush
- a breakfast bowl and spoon
- children's clothing
- shoes
- a large box or basket

I will need

What you do:

1. Discuss your morning routines (see Tips for talk).
2. Examine all the items and talk about their uses.
3. Place all the items in the box or basket and ask the children to take them out one by one and lay them out in order of when they are used.

And another idea:

▶ Using the items above, role play your morning routine. Play 'getting up and getting ready' in the role play or home area of your setting.

Tips for talk:

▶ What do you do as soon as you wake up?
▶ Do you brush or do you comb your hair?
▶ What clothes do you put on first?
▶ Do you like getting up in the morning?
▶ Do you share a bedroom? Who with?
▶ Does anyone help you get ready in the morning?

Following a simple recipe

Recipes aren't just for food! Follow the recipe sequence to make some squishable, rollable dough.

What you need:

▶ ¹/₂ cup of salt
▶ ¹/₂ cup of water
▶ 2 cups of plain flour
▶ 2 tablespoons of baby lotion
▶ a mixing bowl
▶ a wooden spoon
▶ A4 paper or card
▶ ruler and pens or pencils

What you do:

1. Make a recipe sequence card by dividing a sheet of A4 paper or card into six sections.

2. In each section draw the following items: a bowl, flour bag, salt, water, baby lotion, spoon.

3. Prepare all the ingredients and show the children the cards. Explain to them that you would like them to follow the recipe sequence card to make play-dough. Read out these instructions as you hold up each card:

   1. Place the bowl on the table.

   2. Put the flour in the bowl.

   3. Add the salt.

   4. Add the water.

   5. Add the baby lotion.

   6. Mix everything together with the spoon.

4. Once the dough has been vigorously mixed, lift it out of the bowl and show the children how to knead it.

5. Now you're ready to play!

And another idea:

▶ Make instruction picture cards for other simple no-cook recipes such as a sandwich, yoghurt or a fruit salad.

Tips for talk:

▶ What do you like to make with dough?

▶ What does the dough feel like? Can you describe the colour of dough?

The toothbrush boogie (brushing teeth)

Brushing our teeth is something we all should do at least twice a day. Learning a simple action sequence makes developing the habit of a good toothbrushing technique lots of fun.

What you need:

▶ your fingers – for the toothbrushes!

What you do:

1. Talk about the importance of cleaning your teeth thoroughly at least twice a day and what we need to clean our teeth with. Remind the children that it is very important to stand still when we are cleaning our teeth – running with a toothbrush can be dangerous!

2. Recite the 'Toothbrush Boogie' (on the opposite page) and challenge the children to mime the sequence of toothbrushing actions along with you.

Toothbrush Boogie

Pick your toothbrush up
Up up up!
(hold hand up in front of mouth)

Put the toothpaste on
Squeeeeeeze it on!
(mime squeezing toothpaste onto your finger/toothbrush)

Brush it to the left
Round and round
(circular motions in front of mouth, baring teeth)

Brush it to the right
Up and down
(up and down motions in front of mouth, baring teeth)

Are you ready to shout?
NOW RINSE IT OUT!

And another idea:

▶ Toys need clean teeth too. Put toothbrushes in the home area in your setting.

Tips for talk:

▶ Do you like brushing your teeth?

▶ What colour is your toothbrush at home?

▶ Do you like the taste of toothpaste?

▶ What else can we do to look after our teeth?

The great sock race (taking shoes and socks on and off)

Shoes and socks can get children in a tangle. Following instructions in the right order can make sure they put their best foot forward.

What you need:

▶ pairs of children's own shoes
▶ pairs of children's own socks
▶ beanbags – one per child
▶ a large space where the children can safely go barefoot, such as a hall or outdoor grassy area

What you do:

1. Place the beanbags in the centre of the hall or grassy area.
2. Seat the children in a line and ask them to put on their shoes and socks. (If a child is wearing tights give her a spare pair of socks).
3. Tell the children you are going to have a race. When you say 'Go' children race to take off their shoes and socks.
4. They then must pick up a beanbag from the centre, place it between their knees and try to get to the other side of the hall or playground area without dropping it.
5. The winner is the first to make it across the room without dropping the beanbag!

And another idea:

▶ Introduce the concept of a number sequence by decorating pictures of increasing numbers of shoes. Collect 10 pictures of pairs of shoes (catalogues are a good source). Cut out and stick one pair of shoes on the first piece of A4 card, then two pairs on the next, three pairs on the next, and four pairs on the fourth piece of card. Provide the children with collage materials and glue and ask them to decorate the shoes. Place the decorated shoes cards in sequence – the card with one pair of shoes at the beginning, the card with four pairs at the end.

▶ Learn to tie shoelaces using either real shoes or a shoelacing board.

▶ Practise doing up buckles using shoes or belts. Always closely supervise any use of belts.

Tips for talk:

▶ Do you find it tricky or easy to put on your socks?

▶ Where do you sit to put on your socks and shoes?

▶ Do you have a favourite pair of socks? What do they look like?

▶ What are your best shoes?

Topic Three

Growth, development and time

Our knowledge and understanding of the world we live in, and the way we live in it, is shaped by sequences, from the sequences of growth and development of animals, people and plants, to the way we understand time. This section contains activities that cover these important early years topics.

- ▶ Tadpoles to frogs
- ▶ Kittens and cats
- ▶ Cress heads (plant lifecycles)
- ▶ Babies to grandparents (human development)
- ▶ One day at nursery
- ▶ Seasons of the year

Tadpoles to frogs

Animal life cycles create fascinating sequencing activities. Make these tadpole sequencing cards and discover the exciting journey from frogspawn to frog.

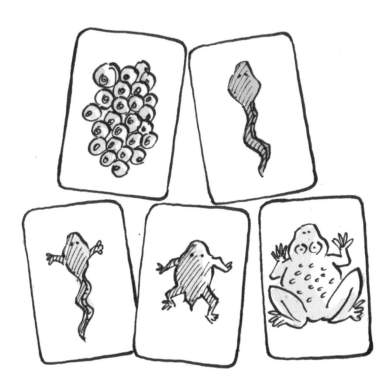

What you need:

▶ card
▶ felt tip pens: brown, black and green
▶ scissors

What you do:

1. Cut out five squares of card (8cm x 12cm)
2. Draw the basic five stages of a frog's development from a tadpole on each card:

   1. Frogspawn,

   2. A tadpole,

   3. A tadpole with legs and a tail,

   4. A tadpole with no tail, front and back legs and a greener colour,

   5. A fully developed frog.

   If you are not confident about your drawing skills source and print out photos from a website.
3. Talk through the life cycle of a frog with children as you show children the cards (see Tips for talk).
4. Now show the children the cards in random order. Ask them to sequence the cards.
5. Discuss their choices. Do you all agree?

And another idea:

▶ Look on the internet with the children at photographs of frogspawn, tadpoles and frogs.

Tips for talk:

Talk about the life cycle of a frog:

1. Frogs lay eggs. This is called frogspawn. Frogspawn is a collection of clear jelly-like eggs. In the middle of each clear egg is a little black dot. That dot is going to be a tadpole.
2. Each dot grows into a tadpole. At first a tadpole has just a body and tail.
3. It then grows legs, and loses its tail.
4. The legs get larger and the body changes colour and shape.
5. Finally the tadpole changes into a frog. It can now spend time on land as well as in water.

Kittens and Cats

Many children observe the growth and development of pets in their homes or the homes of family and friends. This simple cutting and sticking activity encourages children to not only develop the fine motor skills associated with scissor grip but also to understand growth and development in animals.

What you need:

► assorted pictures of kittens and cats (you could ask the children to bring in photos of their pets or you can obtain lots of very cute pictures from books or online)

► A4 sugar paper or thin card (enough for one per child)

► glue and spreaders or brushes

► scissors

► woollen pom poms

What you do:

1. Discuss the ways in which animals change as they get older (see Tips for talk).

2. Look at the photos of the kittens and cats you have collected. Ask the children to tell you which ones are kittens and which ones are cats.

3. Help the children to fold a sheet of A4 card in half.

4. Ask the children to choose one favourite picture of a kitten and a favourite picture of a cat.

5. Children now glue their two pictures – one on each half of the card. The kitten is on the left, the cat is on the right.

6. Children then decorate their card with the woollen pom poms.

And another idea:

▶ Play kittens and cats: Children run around the room (or outdoor area). When you say 'Kittens!', children roll and bound about on all fours. When you say 'Cats!' they stop still and mime washing behind their ears.

Tips for talk:

▶ Do you have a pet?

▶ Did you get him/her when he/she was young?

▶ How has he/she changed as he/she got older? How are kittens different from cats?

▶ What do kittens like to play with?

Cress heads (plant life cycles)

Quick and easy-to-grow cress shows children the sequence of growth from seed to plant.

What you need:

- cress seeds
- cotton wool
- kitchen towel
- clean and empty cardboard egg cartons
- scissors

I will need

What you do:

1. Talk about the development of seeds to plants (see Tips for talk).
2. Carefully cut the top off the egg boxes leaving only the base.
3. Show the children how to fill the egg boxes with dampened kitchen towel and top with damp cotton wool.
4. Now ask the children to sprinkle over the cress seeds.
5. Place the egg boxes in a warm area e.g. above a radiator.
6. Observe the growth each day. Note and discuss the changes in appearance. You could use a notebook.
6. Add one more step to the sequence – harvesting – and make yourself some cress sandwiches for tea!

And another idea:

▶ Plant other seeds according to season. Sunflowers can be grown in small pots inside and then potted up in the summer and placed in your setting's outside area.

▶ If you are lucky and have a garden, plant a crop such as corn. If you have a wild area scatter wildflower seeds to attract some minibeasts!

Tips for talk:

▶ What do plants need in order for them to grow?

▶ What other animals need water?

▶ What do you think the plant roots do?

Babies to grandparents (human development)

Introduce children to the changes that take place as we age by making a picture timeline together.

What you need:

▶ Multiple pictures of people of all ages from babies to the elderly (include babies, different aged children, teenagers and different aged adults)

▶ Long roll of backing paper – lining paper or wallpaper are ideal.

I will need

What you do:

1. Talk about the differences in appearance between young people and older people. (Grit your teeth and smile if children mention your wrinkles!)

2. Display the images and discuss them. Ask the children what the possible ages of the people in the pictures are.

3. Now, make a people timeline. Ask the children to place the babies at one end of the roll and the oldest people at the other.

4. Now discuss where the other people should go on the timeline.

5. When everyone is happy with the order, glue the pictures in place and display on your wall.

And another idea:

▶ Ask the children to bring in pictures of their parents, grandparents or carers as children and/or pictures of the children themselves as babies.

Tips for talk:

▶ What do babies wear?

▶ What can you do that babies can't do?

▶ What can you do when you are older that you can't do now?

▶ What do you want to do when you are grown up?

One day at nursery

Help children to think about and record the structure of the day in your setting.

What you need:

▶ a digital camera
▶ a printer/laminator
▶ a cork board
▶ pin tacks (adult supervision needed) or sticky tack

What you do:

1. In preparation for this activity, take photos of the children engaged in activities at different times of the day: hanging coats, sitting on the mat, choosing activities, eating snacks and lunch, at story time and at pick up time. Print out the photos and laminate if possible. (You may already have a selection of photos that can be used for this activity.)

2. Talk to the children about what happens during a session in your setting (see Tips for talk).

3. Show them the photos – they will be very interested to see themselves and their friends! Examine them together and discuss what is going on in each photo.

4. Ask children to choose the photo that shows something that takes place first thing in the day and stick or pin it at the top of the board.

5. Then ask them to choose what happens next and stick or pin that photo to the board and so on until all the photos are stuck on the board, from the first to the last activity of the day.

6. Mount the board on a wall for children and parents to look at.

And another idea:

▶ Make a photo diary of a day in your setting. Laminate and display the book to encourage discussion.

Tips for talk:

▶ What do you do when you arrive?

▶ What do you do before you go home?

▶ What is your favourite time of the day?

Seasons of the year

The seasons are a perfect topic for children to learn about the sequence of time. Make a carrot print picture showing the changes in a tree's appearance through the seasons.

What you need:

▶ large sheets of paper – one per child
▶ paint – greens, browns, reds and yellows
▶ carrots
▶ a black felt tip marker
▶ a sharp knife (adult use only)
▶ aprons

What you do:

1. Talk about how trees change through the seasons (see Tips for talk).

2. Fold each piece of paper in half lengthways, then in half again so that you have four equal sized sections.

3. With the black marker draw a simple outline of a tree in each of the sections. Each tree represents a season. You may now want to photocopy this sheet for more groups.

4. Cut a carrot in half. The two cut ends will be the printing surfaces.

5. With the tip of the knife score cut lines into the carrots so that they resemble leaf veins.

6. Ask the children to work in groups and print a few light green leaves on the spring tree, lots of green leaves on the summer tree, brown, red and yellow leaves on the autumn tree, and leave the winter tree bare.

And another idea:

▶ Collect autumn leaves and make collages with them.

▶ If you have a tree in your outdoor area take a series of photographs of it as it changes through the year.

▶ Use other vegetables to make prints. Cauliflower and broccoli make interesting leaf patterns.

Tips for talk:

▶ Discuss the changing appearance of trees during the year: Trees come into bud in the spring; they are covered in green leaves in the summer; in the autumn leaves turn brown, red and gold and in the winter they fall to the ground.

▶ Do you have trees near your house?

▶ What animals live in trees?

Topic Four

Physical development and movement

Gross and fine motor skills are practised through sequencing skills, whether used during construction activities, during travelling movements or games, or during fine motor activities such as cutting or threading.

▶ Simon says sequences

▶ Totem poles (threading patterns)

▶ Crazy caterpillars (threading patterns)

▶ Tall towers

▶ Follow the connecting block road

Simon says sequences

This is an adaptation of the game 'Simon says' but instead of one action being called for, give a short sequence of actions.

What you need:

▶ space to stand and move around freely

What you do:

1. Ask the children to stand in a space. Make sure there is plenty of room to move around.

2. Warm up by familiarising yourselves with parts of the body. Can you touch your head? Your nose? Your tummy? Your toes?

3. Now say 'Simon says' and give a sequence of two or three instructions, For example: Simon says... touch your knees, your nose, your knees. Simon says ... touch your head, your chin, your shoulders. And so on.

4. Add other movements into the sequence such as hop, skip, jump, forward roll, star jump, bunny hop, etc.

5. How long a sequence of actions can you remember? Can anyone remember five, or even six?

Totem poles (threading patterns)

Follow pattern sequencing cards to create colourful totem poles using pipe cleaners and beads.

What you need:

▶ large pipe cleaners
▶ plasticine, dough or modelling clay
▶ a large selection of coloured beads with large holes (5 different colours)
▶ thin card
▶ 5 coloured pens or felt tip makers that match the colours of the beads
▶ scissors, pencil and ruler

What you do:

1. First, create pattern cards by cutting the thin card into strips (4cm x 10cm). Make enough for one per child.

2. Divide each strip into five 2cm blocks.

3. Create a sequence of five colours by colouring in the 2cm blocks with felt tips/colouring pens. Laminate if possible.

4. To make the totem pole start by making the base of your totem with a large blob of plasticine, dough or modelling clay.

5. Fold a pipe cleaner in half and twist to make it thicker, and push the end of the pipe cleaner into the base. Make enough poles for each child.

6. Give each child a pattern card, a totem pole and a selection of beads.

7. Place the card vertically in front of them and challenge them to match the pattern on the card by threading the same colour pattern of coloured beads onto their totem pole.

And another idea:

▶ Make a giant totem pole wall picture using a repeated sequence. You could use: photocopies of images, children's handprints, natural materials or fabric.

Tips for talk:

▶ Look at and discuss pictures of Native American totem poles online or in books.

▶ Can you see animal faces? Totem poles are often named after animals.

▶ What kind of animal totem pole would you like to see?

Crazy caterpillars (threading patterns)

This activity is more challenging than 'Totem poles' as children are required to make sequences of 6.

What you need:

- ▶ threading string
- ▶ a large selection of coloured beads and buttons (six different colours)
- ▶ googly eyes
- ▶ pattern sequencing cards (see opposite for instructions)
- ▶ scissors and a ruler
- ▶ 6 coloured pens or felt tip markers that match the colours of the beads

What you do:

1. First, create pattern cards by cutting the thin card into strips (4cm x 12cm). Make enough for one per child.
2. Divide each strip into six 2cm blocks.
3. Create a sequence of six colours by colouring in the 2cm blocks with the colouring pens. Laminate if possible.
4. To make the caterpillar, provide each child with a pattern card, threading string, and a selection of coloured beads.
5. Place the card horizontally in front of them and challenge them to match the pattern on the card by threading the same colour pattern of coloured beads onto the string to make a caterpillar.
6. Stick the googly eyes on the first bead and help the children to tie a knot at the end of the last bead.

And another idea:

▶ Make a caterpillar challenge. How long can you make your caterpillar? How many times can you repeat the sequence on your pattern card?

▶ Make more crazy caterpillars using other threadable items such as cotton reels, clean, pierced milk bottle tops or woollen pom poms.

▶ Read 'The Very Hungry Caterpillar' by Eric Carle.

Tips for talk:

▶ What do caterpillars like to eat?

▶ How do caterpillars move?

▶ What does a caterpillar turn into?

Tall towers (construction play)

Whether you are constructing tall towers or a small garden shed, instuctions have to be followed!

What you need:

- ▶ thin card
- ▶ five different coloured pens
- ▶ scissors and a ruler
- ▶ box of wooden or plastic blocks in the same five colours as the coloured pens

What you do:

1. First, create pattern cards by cutting the thin card into strips (4cm x 10cm). Make enough for one per child.

2. Divide each strip into five 2cm blocks.

3. Create a sequence of five colours by colouring in the 2cm blocks with the felt tips/colouring pens. Laminate if possible.

4. Seat the children on the carpet area and give each child a pattern card and provide the box of bricks for them to choose from.

5. Now challenge the children to make a high tower following the colour sequence on their card.

6. Can they see how many times they can repeat the pattern to make a very very tall tower?

7. Always remember to smile as the tower falls – it is part of the fun!

And another idea:

▶ Use different pattern cards to make several towers next to each other. Can you join them at the top?

▶ Use long bricks to make a series of coloured bridges.

▶ Allow children plenty of time to explore construction play independently.

Tips for talk:

▶ Have you seen builders working? What were they building?

▶ What kind of tools do builders use?

▶ If you live in a tower how do you get to the top?

Follow the connecting block road

Make a multi-coloured road that leads to an exciting place...

What you need:

- ▶ thin card
- ▶ scissors and a ruler
- ▶ five different coloured pens
- ▶ a box of connecting blocks in the same five colours as the coloured pens
- ▶ small world buildings (optional)

What you do:

1. First, create pattern cards by cutting the thin card into strips (4cm x 10cm). Make enough for one per child.

2. Divide each strip into five 2cm blocks and create a sequence of five colours by colouring in the 2cm blocks with the felt tips/colouring pens. Laminate if possible.

3. Ask the children to make a colourful brick road following the colour sequence on the card.

4. Challenge them to see how many times they can repeat the pattern to make a really long road! Can they make it turn corners?

5. Place small world buildings around your road.

Art and design

As any creative practitioner knows, making a work of art whether it be painting, sculpture or collage, involves a series of steps. Children in the early years can practise a wide range of skills while involved in the creation of art and design, from planning and creating, to final execution. Fine motor skills, mathematical skills, and ideas of cause and effect are all involved in the sequences in the following activities:

▶ Making a sandcastle

▶ Making a doughman

▶ Rose collage

▶ Lava-rama

Making a sandcastle

Make these super sandcastles in the sand area in your setting.

What you need:

- card
- pens
- a sand pit or sand box
- buckets and spades
- water (to dampen sand)
- flags

What you do:

1. Make a sequencing card by dividing the card into six equal sections (as in previous activities).
2. Illustrate the following instructions – one per section:

   1. A bucket and spade,
   2. Sand being scooped into the bucket with the spade,
   3. Small amount of water being poured into bucket,
   4. An upturned bucket with hand patting the base,
   5. Hands carefully lifting the the bucket off to reveal the moulded sancastle,
   6. Sandcastle with a flag stuck in the top.

3. Talk about making sandcastle (see Tips for talk).
4. Show the children the sequencing card and resources and discuss the steps to make the sandcastle.
5. Allow children plenty of time to experiment and enjoy making the sandcastles!

And another idea:

▶ Decorate your castle in a sequenced pattern of shells or sparkly jewels.
▶ Build a moat around the castle.

Tips for talk:

▶ Have you ever made a sandcastle at the beach?
▶ What do you think sand is made from? Research and discuss how sand is made.

Making a doughman

Follow the sequencing card to make a doughman!

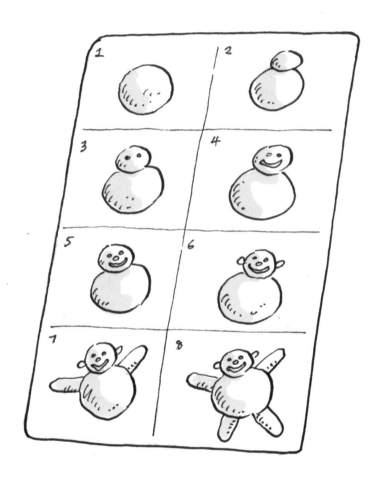

What you need:

▶ thin card
▶ pens
▶ dough
▶ dough cutters and rollers

I will need

What you do:

1. Make the sequencing card by dividing the card into 8 equal sections.

2. Draw the following image – a different one in each section:

   1. Circular body,

   2. Head and body,

   3. Head, body and eyes,

   4. Head, body, eyes and mouth,

   5. Head, body, eyes, mouth and nose,

   6. Head, body, eyes, mouth, nose,

   7. Head, body, eyes, mouth, nose and arms,

   8. Head, body, eyes, mouth, nose, arms and legs.

3. Talk to the children about making a snowman (see Tips for talk). Tell them they are going to make a doughman!

4. Display the sequencing card you have made. Talk through the stages.

5. Give each child a copy of the card and some dough.

6. Ask the children to follow the instructions and make their doughman.

And another idea:

► Make a snowman out of dough.

► Make a snowman collage. Follow the sequencing card and cut and stick fabric, coloured paper, or other suitable material to make a snowman picture.

Tips for talk:

► Have you ever made a snowman? What do you do first?

Rose collage

Creating a collage provides an excellent opportunity to practice sequencing skills. Layer brightly coloured circles in order of size to make these gorgeous blooms.

What you need:

▶ thick card and paper in a variety of colours
▶ backing card
▶ glue
▶ scissors
▶ green and brown coloured pencils

I will need

What you do:

1. Look at photos of a wide variety of different colours and sizes of roses (use books or the internet).

2. Draw 4-6 circles of decreasing size on different coloured card. Draw around circular templates to keep the sizes consistent.

3. Cut out the circles.

4. Support children in making a rose collage by gluing the largest circle on a piece of background paper, then gluing the second largest on top.

5. Continue gluing the other circles, one on top of the other, from largest to smallest.

6. Ask the children to draw stems and leaves to complete their rose.

And another idea:

▶ Using sticky tape, fix your paper roses to thin wooden sticks. Place a lump of florists' foam in the base of a small flower pot and 'plant' your flowers.

▶ Why not make a fabulous window box or create a table display for children to take home?

Lava-rama

Make an awe inspiring volcano by cutting and sticking layers of fiery tissue paper in the right order. Watch out below!

What you need:

▶ backing paper

▶ brown card

▶ yellow, orange, and red tissue paper

▶ glue and scissors

▶ sticking tape

What you do:

1. Using the brown card, cut out a cone shape. Trim the top point to create a volcano shape and use the sticking tape to hold the card together.

2. Glue the base of the volcano to a piece of backing paper.

3. Now ask the children to follow this colour sequence to make the lava: Red. Orange. Yellow.

4. Support the children to cut out and stick long strips of red tissue paper to the sides of the volcano.

5. Now ask them to cut out and stick shorter strips of orange tissue on top of the red.

6. Finally ask them to cut out and stick short, thin strips of yellow tissue on top of the orange.

7. Glue the orange and yellow layers at the top end only so that the top layer of lava can move and flow!

And another idea:

▶ Make a volcano and layers of lava out of clay, then bake and paint.

▶ Add the volcanos to small world play.

Tips for talk:

▶ Look at pictures of volcanoes online. What is lava made from?

▶ Why are there volcanoes on our planet?

Music and dance

Music and dance are both made up of sequences. Dance is a sequence of body movements. Children love to learn dances and even the youngest children can follow a simple sequence especially if they are part of a song. While dance is a sequence of movements, music is a sequence of sounds or notes played rhythmically. The activities in this section cover sequencing skills to be explored in music, action songs and dance.

▶ Teddy bear, Teddy bear (and other action songs)

▶ Dot-dot-dash

▶ Let's make a band!

▶ The hand jive

▶ Travelling dance – moving across the floor

Teddy bear, Teddy bear (and other action songs)

Children will love following the sequence of actions in these popular rhymes.

What you need:

▶ good, strong voices!

▶ space for everyone to jump and move around

I will need

What you do: —————————————————

1. Chant this song and perform the actions. Perform the actions clearly and distinctly:

Teddy Bear, Teddy Bear

Teddy bear, Teddy bear
Turn around.
(walk in a small circle)
Teddy bear, Teddy bear
Touch the ground.
(touch the ground)
Teddy bear, Teddy bear
Turn out the light.
(reach up with hand and press switch)
Teddy bear, Teddy bear
Wave goodnight!
(wave)

2. Can you think of other actions for the teddy bear to perform? Could he... stand on the stair, brush his hair, eat his tea, bend his knee?

3. Now try these fun action songs with sequenced actions:

Five speckled frogs

Five little speckled frogs
(hold 5 fingers up)
Sat on a speckled log
Eating the most delicious bugs
(mime eating bugs)
Yum Yum!
(pat tummy)
One jumped into a pool
(jump)
Where it was nice and cool
Now there were only four
(hold four fingers up)
(Repeat the verse with 4, 3, 2 frogs until there is only 1 frog left, 'Now there was only one!')

Five big peas

Five big peas in a pea pod pressed,
(children hold up hand in a fist)

one grew, two grew, so did all the rest.
(put thumb and fingers up one by one)

They grew and grew
(raise hand in the air very slowly)

and did not stop. Until one day the pod went POP!
(clap hands together sharply)

Head, shoulders, knees and toes

(Point to the parts of the body in sequence)

Head, shoulders, knees and toes,
knees and toes.

Head, shoulders, knees and toes,
knees and toes.

And eyes and ears and mouth and nose...
Head, shoulders, knees and toes,
knees and toes!

(Now repeat, faster!)

Dot-dot-dash

Predict and reproduce this simple rhythmic pattern of fast and slow beats by following a sequence of long and short lines.

What you need:

- ▶ a white board or chalk board
- ▶ whiteboard pens or chalks
- ▶ beaters and drums – one for each child

I will need

What you do:

1. Explain to the children that a drawn dot represents a sharp, quick beat. A dash represents a long beat.

2. Let the children practise making short quick beats and long slow beats with the beater and drum.

3. Draw two dots and a dash on the board and lead the children to follow that sequence. Say 'quick, quick, slow' as you do so.

4. Draw two dashes and three dots on the board. Help the children to follow the sequence. Say 'slow, slow, quick, quick, quick.'

5. Have fun experimenting with creating other rhythm patterns.

And another idea:

▶ Make your rhythm section into a performance, perhaps for a festival or, if you are part of a larger school, for an assembly.

Let's make a band!

Play a sequence of sounds using three different instruments.

What you need:

▶ chimes
▶ drums and beaters
▶ shakers
▶ large flash cards

I will need

What you do:

1. Make a set of three large flash cards; one has a picture of a chime on it, one has a picture of a drum on it and one has a picture of a shaker on it. Draw or find images online.

2. Organise children into three groups of three – 'the chimers', 'the drummers' and 'the shakers'.

3. Give each group either a set of chimes, drums or shakers (one per child).

4. Tell the children that they will play their instruments following the sequence of the flash cards.

5. Now display the flash cards showing a sequence for the children to follow, e.g. if the chime card, shaker card and drum card are displayed this is the order that the groups should play their instruments.

6. Practise playing the sequence and then change the order (sequence) of the flash cards to create a new piece of music!

And another idea:

▶ Let children play their own group 'three instrument sequence'. Make duplicate flash cards by photocopying the images you have drawn (or cut out) for the activity above. Make enough for one set per group of three children. Give each group of three children a different instrument to play. Display different variations of the cards for children to follow.

▶ Instead of instruments, teach children a sequence of body pops to make a sequence of dynamic sounds. Start with a simple stamp - clap sequence: stamp - clap - stamp - clap. Then try a more complex sequence to include knee slaps, e.g. stamp - clap - slap - slap - clap - stamp.

The hand jive

The hand jive was a popular form of dance in the 1950s. If there was no room to dance, people could dance, or 'jive', with their hands instead!

What you need:

▶ Suitable music to jive to!

What you do:

1. To perform this simple hand jive you need to master three simple moves.

   ▶ Slap knees
   ▶ Hand clap
   ▶ Thumbs up over shoulder

2. To perform the jive, seat the children either on chairs or on the floor.

3. Show them the sequence of moves:

   ▶ Slap knees twice
   ▶ Clap hands twice
   ▶ Thumbs up twice

And another idea:

▶ Develop some different moves such as cross hands one over the other, make fists and bump one on top of the other, wiggle fingers, hand to opposite elbow and circle index finger.

▶ Can the children create an extended sequence with these moves?

Travelling dance – moving across the floor

In the past many formal dances involved travelling across a floor using a repeated sequence of steps.

What you need:

▶ a large space

What you do:

1. Teach the sequence of dance steps to the children.

   The moves:

   ▷ Wiggle (wiggle your whole body)

   ▷ Stretch (arms up high, wave hands)

   ▷ Step (take one step).

2. Then put the moves together into a dance.

   ▷ Wiggle and stretch

   ▷ Wiggle and stretch

   ▷ Three steps forward wiggle and stretch

   ▷ Repeat.

3. Replace three steps forward with three steps back.

4. Chant this rhyme as you dance to help you remember the sequence:

   ▷ Wiggle and stretch

   ▷ Wiggle and stretch

   ▷ 1, 2, 3 wiggle and stretch.

And another idea:

▶ Create travelling dance sequences of your own.

▶ Keep the sequences short and simple and repeat with minor variations so that travel happens in more than one direction.

▶ Watch videos of ballroom dances such as the waltz, foxtrot and polka.

The Little Books series consists of:

All Through the Year

Bags, Boxes & Trays

Big Projects

Bricks and Boxes

Celebrations

Christmas

Circle Time

Clay and Malleable
Materials

Clothes and Fabrics

Colour, Shape and Number

Cooking from Stories

Cooking Together

Counting

Dance

Dance, with music CD

Discovery Bottles

Dough

Drama from Stories

50

Explorations

Fine Motor Skills

Fun on a Shoestring

Games with Sounds

Growing Things

ICT

Investigations

Junk Music

Kitchen Stuff

Language Fun

Light and Shadow

Listening

Living Things

Look and Listen

Making Books and Cards

Maps and Plans

Making Poetry

Mark Making

Maths Activities

Maths from Stories

Maths Outdoors

Maths Songs and Games

Messy Play

Minibeast Hotels

Music

Nursery Rhymes

Outdoor Play

Outside in All Weathers

Parachute Play

Persona Dolls

Phonics

Playground Games

Prop Boxes for Role Play

Props for Writing

Puppet Making

Puppets in Stories

Resistant Materials

Role Play

Sand and Water

Science through Art

Scissor Skills

Sewing and Weaving

Small World Play

Sound Ideas

Special Days

Stories Fom Around The
World

Storyboards

Storytelling

Seasons

Time and Money

Time and Place

Traditional Tales

Treasure Baskets

Treasureboxes

Tuff Spot Activities

Washing Lines

Writing

Woodwork

All available from
www.bloomsbury.com